PAN DAIMONIUM

Poems by

Nanos Valaoritis

ISBN: 0-9679315-7-6

Library of Congress Control Number:
200411720

Philos Press

8038-A N. Bicentennial Loop SE
Lacey, Washington 98503
www.philospress.org
info@philospress.org

ACKNOWLEDGEMENTS

Some of these poems have been published in *Beatitude, Exquisite Corpse, Kayak,* the *Milano Poesia Catalogue* (1987) and *Poly* (1989), published in memory of Bob Kaufman.

"The Birth of Second Sight" was published in *Diplomatic Relations* (Panjandrum Press, 1972).

DIOTIMA: So you see you are a person who does not consider Love (Eros) to be a god.

SOCRATES: What then I asked, a mortal?

DIOTIMA: Anything but that.

SOCRATES: Well what then?

DIOTIMA: As I previously suggested, between a mortal and an immortal.

SOCRATES: And what is that Diotima?

DIOTIMA: A great Daimon, Socrates, for the whole of the Daimonic is between the divine and the mortal.

SOCRATES: Possessing what power?

DIOTIMA: Interpreting and transporting human things to the gods and divine things to humans ... and whosoever has skill in these matters ... (prophecy, prayers, etc.) is a wise daimonic man ... and these daimons are many and of all kinds, so Eros is one of them.

Plato: Symposium

CONTENTS

UNTITLED

For many years I have pursued a poem
Which regularly escapes me
It's a funny little poem
About nothing at all
If I remember well
Such as those written today
And cleverly crafted to say nothing
Yet this little poem became a hole
In my life: a small black hole
Out of which poured nothingness
And — invaded me, slowly
With its deadly darkness
While I stood there steadfast
Holding on for dear life
To the sinking twilight
And now it's too late
To remember anything
About this empty spot
This grain of something greater
Than anything in the universe.

THE BIRTH OF SECOND SIGHT

With great difficulty I manage to get out of my skin
After some hair-raising moments everything goes smoothly
My arm is now fully disengaged and I lift myself literally
Out of myself by deftly inserting my liberated finger
Between my shoulder and the lining beneath the muscle
I pull and push and slowly but surely it slides out
The opening is now big enough for the head
A quick tug is all it takes and I am out
What an amazing purity of consciousness
What an experience to see the world
Without the self's enveloping atmosphere
Everything is trembling with transparent colour
Women's thoughts are readable as the daily paper
The minds of little children contain untold marvels
The men magnificent like painted savages
The trees a patch of liquid green flowing
Into the earth's hands holding the sky's vessel
I am squeezing the rest of me out
At last I am free of myself as I have never been before
Now I can see who was this other me I heard so much about
A pure structure of thoughts sensations and emotions
Built inside a body of words with intervals
As vast as the stars of a galaxy
Against the blackness of eternal silence

The Birth of Second Sight

INVISIBLE POEM

I rejoice over our scattered life
What life has not been shattered once at least
Young again in the old days looking for shells
The seaside entered into a basket
Taken back to town in an automobile
There are things left unused on the table
There are things left unsaid in the cupboard
The wind makes the curtains flutter
The birds give a sour look — at the rising sun
The window has no teeth (so) to speak of
Beyond that everything flows smoothly on the river
Memory is a small gap here on the threshold
At four o'clock that very same day
One afternoon in some faraway country
Tragedy breaks out of a gaping hole in the wall
Inside the sacred skull of a matronly worm
Shrill prediction enters with needlework on its arm
Counter clockwise rose the moon housing words
To gravitate from mouth to ear
Setting your hopes on all fours and
Upon him that packed up the world
You have to become accustomed to find the light
As once only darkness was feared to rest
I came by to say nothing matters
It was in this place — the table had been overturned by the weather
The plates were scattered on the floor
And some knives still sticking on the brown doors
The handles all broken and smattered with love.

AMUSEMENT PARK

The zig-zag of thoughts in your head
The unrolled carpet of waves
The nervous twitch of a stare

The remainder editions of publishers
The long undulating massage
The fin-like conception of purity

The endless regard for the deaf
The fearful attention to sounds
And to those who are blind to all noise

The rumour of faithful emotions
The mystery of threatened relations
The pictures that cling to reality

The unseen made pregnant by looking
The concrete assaulting the abstract
The din of collapsing ideas

In the tongue of fiery conviction
The indirectness aimed at the heart
Of a latitude latched-on to the past

So never be less or more careful
Of the hugeness of separate wills
Colliding like trains in the dark

Observe this delicate skin
Attempting to end its own life
Since the plague turned its back on the country

In a hole where darkness resides
In the pit of a feverish anthill
The echoes of wrong become right

GLADIOLAS

Gladiolas will rise again
To violate regulations
To pump out perfumes
To purify loose ends
To make things soar
To freeze and sneeze me out

Presumably you are dead
But we are not sure
We have to zero your head
For thoughts your heart
For feelins yer mind
For shoes yer hands
For pencils yer eyes
For ties yer nose for toes
yer ears for seas
yer mouth for words
yer tongue for sweets
yer tits for pleasure
yer moons for something
yer sometin sumptin for sumptin else
and we come to the conclusion
that year in and yer out
yer not what yer should have bin
dead or alive

Will gladiolas rise again
and touch heaven with their lips
will the end of the sea occur
in our life time?

Fall, 1979

CHEESE

Suppose a friend knocks on your door and says in the middle of the night: You have to help me. I must find this cheese. If I don't find this cheese I don't know what will happen. I may die. I may become crazy or I may kill someone. So you say, All right man. I have your cheese right here. And you offer him some sharp yellow cheddar or jack cheese. And he says that's not it — Then you say — all right — where can we find it at this hour. In the all night grocery on Pink Street. So you drive him to Pink Street and he gets his cheese. And he's as happy as Larry with his cheese on his lap. And when you get home, he says, All right now for the cheese. I'm fine... Thanks, goodnight. And you go back to your bed wondering why he had been so fixed on a cheese. And you go to sleep and you have the following dream: The cheese is growing. It's an enormous cube that takes up all the room, and your friend is embedded in the cheese half in, half out. He cries to you for help. Save me from the cheese, I'm dying, and you draw your revolver and you kill the cheese. And you wake up wondering what the heck the cheese meant in the dream...

1979

IN THE END

I usually charge without warning
My victim is sent a bill
In the mail. He never recovers.
My system always works. Except
That in some cases people will
Pay. They even do it promptly.
I'm then baffled by the delay
And have to change my tactics.
So I don't send the bill until
The accumulated charges are so high
That no one can reach them.
Not even Maui, the hero —
Or any other mythological fool.
Superman for instance — Green
Lantern — Spider Man, Wonder Woman.
They all give up — Then I have
A feeling of triumph. It flushes
Through my body like a...
Well let's not talk about that
Since perhaps a member of the
Drug-squad may be around.
By now drugged to death
I manage to raise my little finger
And then it all begins: I mean
The catastrophes in the movie.
Houses burn without fire, continents
Drown without water. People breathe
Without air. Others die without laughing.
Some drown without drinking.
Others eat without swallowing: Some
Look without seeing. Seeing what?
What is there worth seeing any more
Except some beautiful woman
Walking in the corridor and smiling
Even if it is in a hospital
Even if it's a nurse
Even if it's not a human being
Even if it's the end
Or just a little before the end
In other words, the beginning

11/27/80

My System Always Works

PLAYING WITH THE PRETORIAN GUARD

Sibylla knew what she was doing
When she slept with Gaius Camillus Continentus
How could she miss a trick; she told me all
About it at dinner at Chez Personne
But left out some vital information
Which I had to fill in: Markos Paulus
Was in agreement of course with the procedure
I trusted in his horse-sense about matters
Far beyond his ken; he always guessed
Right without knowing why
Long forgotten plots and counter plots
Come back to me as in the fingerprinting night
Someone plays Beethoven's sonata in E minor
And they slam the lid: I'm convinced
That had it been me, I would by now
Have ascended to the throne
Although I was only the 18th
In the line of succession: the others
Fell so thick and fast, I couldn't keep
Count. By the time they reached me
The Empire had already fallen.

2/27/79

THE MEMOIRS OF A SPLIT GROUP

(A Balkan Symphony)

When I came out here to the west in the late sixties I ran into some very fine rascals. All dressed up to go at low prices. There was not much I could do since everything seemed to be centered on me; it's they who got the best part of the bargain, which was no big deal anyway. In those days a dollar was still worth 95 cents. Today it's no more than 55. My childhood in Bukarest was to say the least stormy. I went to study in the University of Beograd. I was fluent in Latin, which helped greatly my advance in Slavic and Arabic languages. My surprise was immense when we were invaded by the Greeks. The Emperor had always coveted Illyria — but the Illyrians themselves, poor people, have only survived biologically in the Yugoslave cultural capsule. My days in Sophia were numbered because I had set out for Istanboul where my old friend from medical school, Ahmed Arslan, had a very beautiful sister. They promised me the sister in exchange for my passport. Turks have some difficulty in getting passports. They cost too much. So I sold my identity (Rumanian then) very cheap and presented myself to the Greek Consulate as a displaced Armenian. They took me in after some questioning. There was no question that I was Armenian of Albanian descent. That didn't matter a bit to them. All they wanted to know was if I had been born in Athens. I named famous princes I had known in Rumania: The Mourouzi, the Cantacouzene, the Callimachi, the Soutso. They all vouched for my good name and character and soon I became the most coveted of all citizenships: Second only to Swiss — Americans in the East. It was at that time, as a medical student in Istanboul, that I met two other medical students who called themselves respectively Tristan Tzara and Eugene Ionesco. I met Ionesco 52 times in the same evening. He always thought I was someone else. In the end he said, It's you again. I thought it was you from the beginning. No, I said, it's me. But I'm never the same twice running. "Si jeune et déjà le même," he murmured and walked away. My South American friends in Istanboul were numerous. As a Grecian spy I had become very popular among the riff-raff who thought I would put them on the payroll for "indecent information" about senators. They knew a lot. But it was expensive. So I made a deal with them. Two scandals a week only for a set price. All this information later fell in the hands of the Germans and that is how they kept Turkey out of the war. My friend Suleiman the Magnificent, as his pals called him, gave a party where I met Nanos Valaoritis, Cyril Connolly and other members of the London intelligentsia — marked off by the Russians as potential fellow-travelers. They were wrong. However I will come to this later.

The best years of my life were spent in Split, near Tito's old house.

1980

BURR

Just a funny little thing that
Happened — I've forgotten what
But I'm not yet on the brink
Of oblivion or Nirvana — but
I still remember being on
A street corner — eager
Excited at lunch time
A two hour break from
Dull Work — Despised
By the career staff
As only a temporary —
"You'll never arrive"
They seemed to say:
"To the high position"
We will occupy in
A number of years
You'll remain down
there smaller
and smaller
until you
will va
nish
alto
ge
th
e
r.

THE BIRTH OF APHRODITE

Sometimes we played bat or rats on the veranda
Shut off the sun in webbed light
The smell of brine came in the sitting room
From the far-away sea voluminous with ships
Rocks formed and dissolved in the morning spray
Is this story about the fig-tree true? Ficus Ruminalis
Sliding downwards — her hands her eyes her mouth
All of her sliding downwards toward the tunnels
Of sand from where she rose to be a hundred times over
And over and over again in the same honey-coloured envelope
The sky lit up with buzzing winglets drops of air
Performing somersaults — as they fell from the high vaulted ceiling
Of solid cerulean with faint archangels tracing
White; hands down: hands up whose got it?
The golden coin came from the chest discovered in the cellar
Caesar's head inverted with distorting edicts
Love on high-heels trips over the islands
And falls headlong with a splash into the deep
Hundreds of human voices
Hundreds of human eyes record, repeat the act.

POEM UNLIMITED

The foreleg of a bowl of soup hits my jaw.
A very rusty joke hits the ceiling.
A couple of shoe-strings make calls on their owner.
The colour on the wall beckons cordially.
A poster walks out on you.
Dyed hair becomes a living flame.
No "elephant" can open a can of "sardines" with his trunk.
New ideals fill up my stomach.
My toes clutch wildly as if they were about to drown.
Nothing looks down on me with a blue grin.
Alarm clocks with shattered teeth pronounce wrong.
Waking up dead is my favourite game.
The occasion calls for an oil-strike.
Electric eel caught up in a fragment of ossified lake.
The colour of your tits glows afar.
Candour wakes up the sleeping corridor with a gentle nudge.
A scene of desolation floats off in the dark.
Your locks lock me out of time.
Forged anonymity is no answer for the first time.
Everyone sings with wax in their ears.
Some are also tied by the throat to the past.
The battered building slowly sinks.
Catcalls wave their plumes from check-points
inside your viewpoint. No laughter follows.
Automobiles turn over on their backsides and play dead.
The independence of twilight. The long prayer of freeways.
Most drivers are not aware of a hole in the sky,

In which all hope imaginable is engulfed.
Strangers come back from abroad,
Breathing new portholes into letter boxes.
Everyone treads on arithmetic.
Squirming coils of sound emerge from the inner ear.
The sanctuaries of toilets are being violated by the opposite sex.
Amazement holds me clasped by the waist.
Amplified light is rowing along the river bank.
Sunlight summons all bulbs to attention.
A green gas escapes from the mouths of orators,
Where a holocaust of words is in the making.
No bowl of rice can save a body of knowledge.
Angry looks carved by fire.

A bronze bust begins a lift-off.
Kindness has handles of ivory.
Scintillating secretaries of space.
Changes are ringing inside my head.
Watermills leave the joyful shoes of a plain chant.
The conversation turns brown with side-burns.
Fireworks build a citadel of kisses.
Orifices leak unlocked quantities of space.
A ship's prow ploughs the frowning hillside.
A chorus of clouds blocks the ears of syllables.
I allowed myself to be caressed by strangers.
They are precocious to the point of courage.
All voices converge on a mid-Atlantic masterpiece.
I hold a meeting in people's eyes.
A martyrdom of smiles faces canonization.
Frequent shudders are spattered on the forecast.
No one will be displayed for their good actions.

I feel I'm not boring enough to be understood.
Anyone can guess underdeveloped hair.
Don't mince your metaphors if you like meat-loaves.
Rinse and shave if you cannot do otherwise.
Outrage is not the only way out of eating. There are others.
If you belong don't stay there too long.
Pull their legs off if you can't stand on them.
Betray before becoming an accessory.
Lower yourself up to the highest standards.
Only smile when taken apart.
Secrets don't count. They only blush if blemished.
The long monotonous silence after noise.
I leap large quantities of myself to hide my concealment.
The dull substance of my spittle travels far without a croak.
Lend me the strong offense that windows in your breast.
Further South, guess what—no islands for sale.
A slice of genius is the onion skin of breathlessness.
A very rusty look hits the meaning.
Perspective travels faster than time.
There were fears for her afterlife.
Gentlemen, we have achieved what nothing else couldn't.
Hence, the great Goethe racked his brains.
The history of emotions is tedious enough without feelings.

Black birthdays cause an apoplectic moratorium.
The fear of words deals with the desire of things.
My eyes sting with the ill at ease that fills the room.
Marginal yes, although not mortal.
Thank you for manipulating ice-stardom to infrequency.
I passed through many Cyranodes of illusion.
The ultimate place is suddenly tyrannical.

Economize without wasting.
This line hovers slightly above the page.
Elevated by enthusiasm it is brought down by shot-gun.
There's nothing better to do, than anticipate.
The stamp of my actions are the warriors of my congregations.
The sun swarms of being able.
Without a guitar tuning remains occult.
I'm not really surprised to see you walking on the stage naked.
Even though you're not really flying as promised.
It's not a sword nor has it been sworn in yet.
All three walls converge to form a myth.
Nothing stands as stiff as some flowers.
To be nourished by thoughts the size of a mushroom.
Great piles of air swallowed by those whom thunder strikes.
What I believe in I have to laugh at if it threatens excellence.
The harpsichord strikes a repellent chord in the heart of prosewriting.
I'd appreciate some pretty face from someone.
Efforts are being made so that neither side will talk,
And not only to each other.
Not everyone is necessarily human.
Centripetal forces began to pull us apart.
Centrifugal forces began to bring us together.
We tend to levitate because we can't walk to the next stop.
It is easier on the whole to be a forerunner, in the aftermath.
Even if dreadful things won't happen you can count on it.
Is it possible to pass on information without eyelashes?
Come what may the road stubbornly lies on its back.
A house lies on its side too tired to stand up.
People are walking on all fours so as not to attract attention.
In a restaurant I order a meal for ten. What happened to the other nine?

A Friend of the Poet

As I enter the fog I discover there's no other madman hidden in it.
He offers me his tongue for half a spoon.
Thanks to him I will be able to cut my discoveries in two.
The feminine and the masculine sides are the least conspicuous.
A blow emerges from the lips of innocence.
A jargon full of animals strikes it rich.
I hear a clatter of overthrown cabbage.
I try to swallow but I'm mistaken. It won't go down.
My hand is glued to a glove I've never worn.
Under the circumstances it is safer to say that there's no latitude left.
As the fog becomes denser and denser it clears away.
The domains of thought are not the same
as the domains of humans.
My luxury has been so distilled, that it displeases me.
He offers me part of himself to throw out of the window.
Was he in his right mind on the left side of his brain?

FLAT SURFACES

The table, the floor
The ceiling, the walls.
The tray, a bread-board,
A window-pane
A metal plate
A calm sea — water
In a glass of water
And what you write
Is as flat as all
These surfaces without
Wrinkles or roughness
Smooth and shining
And boring —

FEEL FREE

Feel free to fall asleep
in my bed stranger
whoever you are
looking for a night's rest
longing for understanding
THE SCAFFOLDING OF MY BEING
is not yet exhausted by study
i will vanish nonetheless
not a jot wiser than before
since we all know that i need
to make an impression on the
diseased continent of our mind
and rid it altogether of parasites
fasting and falling faster and faster into
crime so heinous and rotten that I dare not speak
to anyone about it except to you charming creature
of the depths so gifted so beautiful so talented and wick-
ed that i am now stuck with longer and longer lines of communi-
cation to keep going so feel free to send me anything you
want but i repeat three thousand ships will be the re-
quired minimum for creating an impression on the
lost continent of men or women engaged in
mutual acts of destruction stemming from
mainly a paranoid make-up no psychi-
atrist has been able to explain
in terms that make sense to
the layman or the specia-
list and now there's
no time left for
dabbling with
the unknown
any more
than
bef-
or-
e.

POEM ON BROWN PAPER

Part of a sun emerges
In view of Sandwich
Islands incomprehensible
Rosy cape rounded
Barking stories silence
Some of which hear
Released with thunder

The backtracking moon
Thumbtacks on wallpaper
Shipwreck on ice floor
Speech of educated guesses
Prime time organically
Cancelled in vast quantities
Prehensile eyes view-front

Half sunken ideas test
Final capitulation patrolling
Underground water leaks
Principally seen from above
Geography makes words
Sense incorporated disbelief
Perspective blurred by effect

Cone-like configurations south-east
Funneling thoughts through a tube
Dim welcome plays echo
Made to be round stretches out
Until the eye can see no volcano
Noon slashed past a dash
Precipitous will end somewhere

Coming back on your steps is unlikely
Peregrination of dull wits
Simple minded echoes straight out
Of brute force below furnace
(Managed to slip out of this one)
Concrete absence blurs trinity
By not being there was offered

Often taken for another ride
Instant instead of infant
Too trim to be cancelled

Born to let up in drag
Old cult gives superior
Another chance to bear under
Private conversation volatilized

Concepts prone to discordance
Prime time progresses rough play
Vagabond hems in dress up
Truant plaything in trust
Record winds all the way
up to dusty end; it figures
Ribald aims coincide

Practical joke infusion
Aimed at watering water
Outdistanced by long shot
Semantically unfounded civilian
Thereby ended as much
More of much else in store
Some of it coming up for air

So be it when elsewhere occurs
Deep down nothing else changes
Original depth decentered
Proud to rise up so early
Conception derives a detour de force
Clansmen haul out coincidence
Something smells bad

I don't want to think of it
Come on what did I do?
Simply no one in view for the
Time being is continually long
In doing what could be done in a second
Three rounds before the museum
And afterwards in the afternoon

Samples taken offhand
Handling extremes with bare
Knowledge edged on by desire
Thrusting inside from below
Many feign seeing the sea
Tumbling of walls as in dust
Below to another certainty

Of each and for each and from each
Lingering doubts crowd the entrance
The window was closed as before
The storm that had risen subsides
When we come to all this we all stop
To think is the least of surprises
Why not, said the voice in concealment

The ice slowly melts in the oceans
To reveal is not always so easy
Paradeigmatos charin ya peste mou
Pourtant Monsieur c'est bien simple
And then it resumed with some force
The wind bit the windows with frost
To be weak is to leave in a week

Wrecked by the garbage of trains
Distant thinking of cloud-fronts
Rushing up to the camera
To cement a wonderful feeling
Inert as in hospital beds
I perceive without seeing or hearing
Much of this was written instead

I parlayed till the evening fell through
A gap in the ground freshly opened
Fresh dew consumed in vast quantities
Perhaps the right question
To be heard with a loss of attention
Due in part to similar circumstances
I predict the arrival of ships

With unreasonable manners of thinking
And ground covered and lost
Of nothing much in a manner of speaking
From inside thirsting to see
I get drawn by three horses who speak
So near yet so far from the beach
Because of previous examples

Having been dumped many times
In a previous existence
All morning can froth at the windows

Much else that was useless was needed
To complete the survey of the sea
A style which is much in demand
I ordered some waves in the paint-shop

It became quite impossible to walk
Anyone who didn't wears a smile
Out worn three life times ago and then
Something happened to stop the whatever
Was there where it started — which is
As I assumed it to be a space or a clearing
So densely underpopulated by others

Who come in droves every Sunday
To sup to resist to suppose to sit down
In all directions at once which is true
Of the greatest among them who are
As few as the feud that has kept them apart
By a line that was drawn in the middle
Don't mistake what I say for the truth

Is buried in layers of blue
Much too heavy to put into prose
Of a mythical time that escaped
The name-throwing of outrageous bands
Of people that arrived the weekend
It was loyal as long as it lasted
There's no test to prove you're a genius

Your words will be summoned to claim
The opposite flank of the mountain
To get ahead is not within hearing distance
Of people who flock and disperse
Clouds resembling a project left open
It seems somewhat crowded this morning
No I don't think so, I observe

The meticulous edge of the ocean
Where the domiciles rise up and fall
And the night comes out of the foliage
Mounting the crest of a wave
Too much clarity splashes ashore
Speak of absence of climate and place
Inside a joke attached to a necklace

So often repeated again that it marks
On the tablecloth a stain which grows larger
On every occasion — although
The instinct was squashed long ago
Instant breeze refreshes her face
Summoned by whom the bell tolls
To face the ultimate grace whose
Appearance favors those so inclined.

The infinite mounted on a horse
Stands petrified: Homer disappears on the
Horizon. No one knows why or where or when
It all stood still or when it all started.
Among us many are still undecided
Rather themselves than any — one
Else since we are all barricaded in here
Why bother about what he said?
Why be anguished, confused, why belittle it?
All said and done the countdown has begun.

1980

ONCE HOMER WAS MANY AND NOW HE'S ONLY ME

What numbers of authors stupendous
Fraudulently inserted as investigated
Cryptanalytically by vicious grammar
Original mistakes never made as corrected
The god of enjambements once loved and slew
Carnaval of polysyllabic two liners
The story of the remains being scattered
Among seven cities in all; severed
The head went to Chios the center
The phallus to Delos where it's at,
Chastened by sunshine for onlookers;
The lungs are in Athens; the torso
in Smyrna; the body in Ios; the arms
That wrote, in Ephesos. The legs
Went to the Colophonians; who always
Walk together. I expect sophistry to
Distribute more portions of the body — (the anus
The thighs, the buttocks can be seen
In Cyme). So now he's been dismembered
And thus remembered everywhere...
Rendered whole that is, a body of work —
The computer said yes he was a person.
Secretly the limbs are brought in a place
Where the Homeric festival takes place
In the middle of summer in a house
On the outskirts of the city
On the Island of Kos, where I went

To pay my respects to the master.
There I saw the body intact; plastic
Replicas were made for the visitors
To take home, an arm, a leg, or part of the breast.
Some chose the head; I chose the neck;
Only the phallus was not reproduced;
It had to stay where it was on a stand
In the center of sacred Delos; some say
It was the Phallus that sang and not the throat.
I say they are goats who say this; how can
A phallus sing? With what voice? I ask you?
Yet they firmly believe; and they go at night
When the moon is dark and they wait to hear
The voice of the phallus which they say

The God of Enjambments

Comes out of the balls; the high pitched
Melody rings in their ears for the rest
Of their life, so they claim these oddballs
Of fame and curiosities and sensations —
Not one of whom can say what it sang; how could they?
The singing takes place in their heads
And no Homer are they to give utterance
To great songs; I am going next year
To attend this ceremony and hear for myself
What these idiots claim to be true.
But what if I too will misconstrue and believe
As they do, that I heard his voice in the night
A voice that will follow me like a lamb — all my life?
No, no, I refuse to become the dupe of these
Mystics, these occult minded hare-brained
Fanatics, for whom all this is a cult.

For cults I abhor, although I love
All phenomena; so strengthened with sophistry
I will go and withstand successfully
The test. And I went and I withstood the test.
Although lately, I'm beginning to hear
The voice in my ears that whispers:
Don't be a fool, you are Homer; it's you
Whom I chose to inhabit 3000 years later

WHAT COMES FIRST

For François Dufrêne

Resembling the results of bad eyesight
Multiple devourer of itself and amplifier
Of the chiseled word author of the "Tomb
Of Pierre Larousse" future without a future
Made of senseless anger and lost tempers
A previous line is mirrored in the next

The shaming humiliation erased from memory
Internal scream all I have left to lie upon
As on a marble bed with different veins of colour
Boiling greens or livid yellows drowning
Love-clichés endlessly stretched out
In absolutely smooth Procrustes' bed

A single animal was once in the beginning
White language of infinity despoiled
By thundering oval rhetoric slowly chewing
The fossilized Page of History — extinct colossus
My revenge is on the table signed and stamped
Dripping pen from the outside of cruelty

Red tuft of pubic hair breaking a thousand
Pianos — alchemical hoarseness of stringed music
Associated with the wrong place and the empty glass
Before closing time my writing in English
Forgiven me by local wizards since
A single sound was once in the beginning

.

THE TOWER OF BABEL

When the tower of Babel was (being) built
Many (were) the people that were there
Even if they hadn't anything to do
They were curious to see if God would appear.

I too was (there) in a rowing boat
By the banks of the river Euphrates
I stood shyly (apart) behind the dividing rope
That I might see the face of the Lord.

But no one appeared in the sky
The tower shot up even higher
Until we couldn't see the top of it
Even if we strained most terribly our eyes.

Then suddenly a bell rang and someone
Cried "Lunch" in another tongue
Another cried "déjeuner" and "mangare"
And another said "germa" and "essen,"

And brot and gliep and psomi
And yaourti and trophi and icthys
And another said psari and ornithes
And another said voutyro, butter or beurre.

And they thought that this was the signal
To beat the milkmaid to death
To churn her until she had yielded her butter
From the better part of herself.

And I sat down and wept
Not really knowing why
In my heart I had heard
The unbelievable cry,

That rose from the ranks
Of the workers up there
In the sky the clamour of those
Whose fists towards God rose in anger.

And I held the young milkmaid
Close to my heart and my heart
Was beating as fast as was hers
And I hid beneath the tent of her hair.

Oh glory to the great hunter
Who came from Zaboulon
The great hunter Armando
Toledo Togrul Mirador.

ODE TO HUMIDITY

I got the sun on the telephone.
I see death from a liberated point of view.
Yearning for luxury is only permitted to animals.
In polite society those who echo re-echo.
I hear the age old cry: Herein, begone.
Groans emerge from a half-opened envelope.
We are glittering inside each other.
I observe them making all the wrong movements.
When you come into a room the lights go on.
Better than darkness I can give you the obvious.

Precisely. The angry blue eyed mob of tears
Plagues the innocent gaze with moisture.
How much to reach into the maw of summer?
I see a dissolute hand floating towards the curtains.
Obviously, luminosity has to be re-examined.
Terraces are competing for imported clouds of dust.
The women condensed of all idioms became as sharp as rocks.
A goat's mask entered behind a second thought.
The heat will visit the earth on lizard's feet.

Borrowed words are dancing in the dark throat.
I have come to confess I'm a walking shadow thrower.
It only takes the ominous to advance step by step.
Nothing flows in the arms of danger.
Don't you hear anything? I hear everything.
I wept. Gusts of wind are cast aside on the corners.

Then the shop-windows stood up like one man.
Crafty, arty, cunning and manufactured, I reside in bad taste.
A single breath in the palm of the mouth has another name.
A sentence settled down to become happy.
But haven't we talked about this before?

THE ICE COTTAGE

Coming back to the house after an absence of two months. I try in vain to explain to myself that this is my house. The bed has been slept in. I don't know where anything is anymore. There isn't anything anywhere anyway. No milk, no cheese, no bread — nothing, not even fruit juice. The house slightly stinking of cat food left out too long. Even the cat, usually so familiar, has an alien look. And yet the summer was fine. What am I complaining about? I don't know. It's just a malaise. A sick feeling. I want to go to bed. I want to change the sheets. I don't find any. Even the pillows have dwindled. The room is not itself. Finally after enormous efforts the bed is made. With clean sheets found in the corner of a cupboard. I lie on it. There are no books around. It's like a hotel. I stare at the bare ceiling and I wonder why I left those beautiful carved and painted ceilings — for this cardboard box room. Here in the midst of so much complexity I can't even think straight. Why did I leave the sea to itself and to themselves the mountains? There was clarity where I was a little earlier. Here there is only confusion. Even the cars look like untended animals. The yard is desolate. Time has shifted. The same hours are not at hand. Nothing tragic about this, nothing dramatic. Just sordid, reality, small and mean. What am I doing in this place? Why am I here? In other words, why am I not, not here but somewhere else?

GASP

Ambrosia begins with an A
an eye has two e's to its name
you won't believe this but "I love you"
things are so tight they might be loose
some things knock on the door —
others don't seem to matter —   night
The longer the delay the better it is —   at
precisely precocious and something more   tellers
there was about this a kind of message —   automatic
why do they insist so much instead of   from
taking it into their stride — Who is speaking   withdrawing
Please? Turn left —   risks
what's left — who knows   any
Well — well/easy prey   have
tax criminals   to
and the redundancy   impossible
of language   it
affects everyone   make
 alas   and
 3 top   time
 Level   old
   mafia   the
     were   help
       convicted   to
         for   time
           being   the
             members   all
               of the   does
                 commission   one
                     exercise   what
               must   be

FOR

It's true/there's no such thing/
Before/a certain amount of money/
Curtain raisers/seeing the cheerful
aspect/when it was no fun I said/
Plaster some iron over the wall
Running wild?/Verbatim/Secret
Garden/La Viennoise/Dryer's
Grand opening gambit what
                    For?

THE WORD WAS GONE

The sea was gone
But the bridge was left
The writing was left
On the table
The sun was left
On the table
The paper was gone
But the writing was left
In the bag of tricks
In the satchel
In the opening of the bag
Of the month of September
Then later the month was gone
And the old year began
To be written backwards
Memory of the incident
Was gone — but it stood
Backwards in the minds of those
Whom the people had chosen
The few — the many — the old
Man alone writing on his table
The fire was gone on this
Morning of Spring
The power and the glory
All gone.
The secretary swept the table clean
And made it ready
And you were still
Waiting to be fetched.

1984

MEANWHILE

Illocutionary beings invade my lunch hour. Territories follow. Their nature is to be detected. Close by, the shop has everything we need dead. There is no fire escape for my darling and me. Trapped in each other's arms, the only way out is the way in. The dark is unusable in this context. Such promises are now lavishly made and withdrawn. Meanwhile in New York, brown shoes reflect the yellow tides, empty bottles gather yellow liquids, rival groups maintain precarious levels, concentration plagues studious eyebrows, dogs bark at alienation, mercy shows shadows in reflection, a spinal cord rises to the bottom, the skyline hovers over the homeric crowd, helicopters fly mercilessly in and out of views, love-life posters surpass other standards with their own longevity and vulgarity, elaboration hesitates before better company, instilled with barren moments on high heels, a running commentary keeps wild life in check, help is slow to come in little puffs, kitchen aprons turn blue with tide, compliments are becalmed by tossing seas, deafness assails a narrow passage, remarkable has not been seen at the health spot, heavyweights struggle with bow ties, domestic rules get thrown overboard, stiffness sells salient features, performatory sentences match all pauses, ideas edge faintly forward, feathers fail to meet the standards, money shelves up in shallow waters, wormlike holds out promises in kind, they are never replaced by others, indoors life resembles a cherry orchard, Milliner mulls over cautious kerosene, monarchs slow down to a full stop, dawn ketchups the toothy rhyme, praxis shoulders later than before, doubledeckers masters of martial art, music misses strategems by a single dog, minor footfalls in view of Sandwich, folly discovers static electricity, legs leave leaves to holidays, lemurs light up reasons for rattling, rustler, wrongly accused by scandal is not reached, placards sign up for simulation, comely resembles momentarily in numbers, teabones tollbridge for free change, formica falls in between two stools, erratic rightly accuses wrongly, flimsy fades before breakfast, sunset furnishes fables towards wretched, down up requires similarity of treatment.

SELENA

For Sinclair Beiles

They held onto dear life
To their beloved friend the sea
But the sea was friendly no more
It roared and bellowed bit its teeth
It shook its mane of seaweed fibres
It collided with the stars
It drank its own blood bitterly
From its own blood it made wine
Until the sunset turned green
And the pale white face of Luna
Rose above the jagged mouth of rivers
To receive from the hands of God
The only two left-over winds
Dark prizes of forgotten races —
Unwinding their way across the map
Towards ultimate and cozy bliss
Inside caverns filled with mermaids
He drank his own blood and offered it
To Luna who had by then cast off
Her uniform to take her monthly bath
Surrounded by attendant clouds
With ready sheets made of rain
To wash the ancient goddess dry
So that she could lay once more
All clean and bright over the freshly cut waves.

Toward Cozy Bliss

TRIBUTE TO FREQUENT

He committed a double negative
I had an eye for detail
She committed a crime
Double-talk was frequent in those days
She committed no crime
I had an eye for detail
Double-talk was infrequent those days —
She had no eye for detail
I committed no crime
There were frequent stops
He committed no crime
She was being closely watched
There was double talk spread all over
They committed a double negative
I perform for myself in the evening —
I go into one thing after another —
Offering myself to myself
Catching up with me — from all sides
Different sides of my own self.

1984

THE GREEK BOOK OF THE DEAD

I come from a place
stained by lots of money and rhetoric
one oration destroyed whole
strips of land leaving the battlefield
with chariots hanging up to dry
on the rooftops — they had no time
to lift-off and parade over the
brown hills where the holocaust grew
too sharp to dislodge — but
still as in a dream: an army of
plants advanced from the ceiling
a ceiling of skulls and many more
entering with awe the enormous
walls of the mausoleum furnished
with underfed scripts and ornaments
whose women are evident. Today
no oat-meal — steel-cut art supplies
this much needed fighting flesh
to pass the sentinel whose weight
was to become proverbial: another book
of the dead would be superfluous.
Let's not read; let's listen and look:
Unheard he crept away; but his own
howls triumphed over him smashing
him to bits as he hoarded subjects into fits.

ULTIMA TEXT

Hallo Umberto

In reality I'm an Italian poet, although all my work in Italian remains buried in a mysterious manner. It simply will not see the light. Should I be precise, the light of day? It would be safer to surmise that it has been lost, somewhere between my brain and my arm. An error in transmission? Possibly but not certain... My Italian poems were very classical in form. They formed a veritable Fiore Di Levante, a wreath above a shock of dark hair, my own when I was twenty, and crowned with the illusion of hope. Hope for what? Fame? Naturally... Fama, the goddess who shunned me, although I have often met her in dark alleys visiting secretly the houses of my friends and bestowing on them what she refused me: Her gifts of hearts and coronets, cabbages and kings. In reality I'm a pure Italian. My genealogy goes back to the gothic conquerors of Rome, the Theobaldi... the family of my great grandmother. Once I had seen her, I have to spend the rest of my life looking for someone who resembles her. Soon I am to find her double. I see a resemblance to her in my favourite tree. My tree, my tea-cup, my chair, my life begins to resemble my Italian poems. Positively dolce. Very gentle. Really positively. If x-rayed they can be read... on my eyebrows. On chaos. On the rock of my head. Really. Crowned with the illusion of hope. A pure state of language. Eyes that see everything through green glasses. The sound of creased money falling in the Vesuvius of my throat. Will I ever be able to find someone who resembles me without being myself?

BAITING THE MASTER

Murmur of oncoming waters
The buzz of flies the rush of horsemen
Throw down your hat to the other
The other is arriving late tonight
The other will sit at the table
He/she will cut the bread at the table
He/or it will eat at the table
It will lift its eyes toward wine
A light will shine — it will
Colour the background
Murmur of arriving strangers
Half-awakened by the whispering
Of crowds — the gushing waters
The sound of waters in a case —
Gurgling, rattling at the door
The loose handle handled
Once more I hear the oncoming
Footsteps stopping at the door
I hear the empty voice of the wind
Saying nothing to nobody
Whistling round corners
Whining in the courtyards
Sitting on the tree the noise
Of leaves and trenches cutting
Into the silence of the air
The pitter-patter of tiny feet
In the attic down the stairs
Narrow is the gate
Open it please
Flagrant is the intruder
Burning are his eyes
He is coming to the door
He is opening the gate
I hear the click of the latch
I hear the banging of the closing
Of the gate behind him
The footsteps are approaching
They have reached the threshold
Nobody is related to anything
Will he be able to appear?
Will he always be absent?

Was it my longing for an
Appearance that caused
The noise: Did I imagine
It all inside my head
Was I struck by wonderment
Was I floored by nostalgia
Struck dumb with thinking it was real;
Here is the unknown one
Opening the door — He is here
He is stepping inside. The
House is flooded with tiny
Noises, creaks and pit-patter
Of tiny feet in the attic
My eyes are flooded with light
I am blinded by the light
The unbearable light envelopes my body —
I'm struck dumb by the arrival
Of the night holding a lamp
Looking into my things —
As if I were not there

Short is the nature of light
Long is the nature of darkness
And there is nowhere else to go —
Endless is the waiting
Empty are the words that say
Always forever dearest
We'll be here — we'll be
In each other's arms —
In every possible future
We will inhabit
The little house of our dreams —
Only to vanish in thin air
Empty is the grave
Nobody is there:
Staring at us from black sockets
Watching the passing of the air.

TORNADO

She lay on the edge of a sentence bathed in a purple passage
coloured moments rose to the surface words of another meaning
hidden bubbles below the surface the underside of a paragraph
Invaded by itself slithering in and out of a subject. Queen
Margaret's facial lift carried on through the ages.
Carnivorous I ate all the thoughts I could break
off from the forbidden family tree. Wide open I
wandered over the mudflats admiring the texture
constructed by so many users. The wonder
was no less great than in other circum-
stances would have been the cities.
Only here it took form of an up-
rooted day fertile in hours
returned to its origins
in order to be able
to say eventually
something that
mattered to
nature:
Find me
in here
some
where.

INESTIMABLE

The problem of death
is from what angle you see it —
and that's not all, because
you may see it from the wrong angle
in fact it's the angle with which
one goes out of this world that matters.
If you get out on the right angle
you are delivered — but if you
get out on the previously mentioned one
beware — you'll come bouncing right back
for you will hit the wall of eternal return.

The Problem of Death

IN SEARCH OF THE PRIMORDIAL JOKE

They bring in a covered platter. Expectations rose high. The ladies dressed in their best finery and perfumes, the men in evening clothes. Everyone in a jitter of excitement. They can hardly contain themselves for they are at this point unable to control their eagerness, their anxiety, their impatience to see what is contained in the magical platter which has been brought in with such ceremony by the waiters and the maids. No doubt the platter hides the essence of life — the cake of cakes, the unborn and exquisite taste of tastes. The most rare and special of desserts, which everyone in the room believes they fully deserve for their exertions, for their worth, their sacrifices, their frustrations, their miseries and triumphs. And now, the moment has come to cut the cake, the great undeserved dessert: The hostess stands up with a huge knife in her hand and as she lifts the cover — a gasp runs through the assembly of men and women in evening clothes around the long dinner table. What is revealed is the formless, horrifying shape of an enormous turd.

TRANQUILITY

Mechanical skies reverberate
Ending phrases may reverse
The weather becomes fair
Lighter as the days go by
Wax on candles melts the snow
Background figures light up suddenly
No less than all hands on the seconds
To sink is no big ergo sum
When empty fill up quickly
Remind me of whose speaking
Towards some other sunset
To begin with write carefully
Lay the paper on the ground
"Sorry," was written on the tombstone
Here lies what belies — in what
Principally nothing matters
Make it seem less obvious
Obscurely related comes first
Many stories don't end here
Only the beginning counts
Attempts to show are absolutely nil
I'm not easily fooled by listening
Earlier describes without judging
Pass on the information
I, isn't the faintest idea
Roaring rests its head on its lap
Pillow handles itself deftly

Hair-raising is not only dreamt of
Passively watching those for whom
Merely a flicker of a smile lights up
Read on read on before it's dark
While smiling lips don't ask for more
And thunder is overheard obliquely.

TRIUMVIRATE

So he bent his head and he said
"I'm terribly sorry I rose so high
So to speak so as to impose
Upon all of you this only head

Of mine that now alas must part
From mine and my other parts
Though on a man that's tall it once stood
And moderately by all understood"

In other respects however his breeches
Only reached his knees that were
Halfway between his feet and his arse
Even if he himself never switches allegiance

To those illustrious family witches
Named with an alarming rate
The requests of who-dunit to feed
All the remarkable men whom I've met

And nobody answered the question except what
(In a whisper, in secret, in shame to reveal
Our only adored and beloved adept
However inept — will pretend to conceal)

To fend off brutal remarks on the fact
Of not having an inkling of tact
By revealing a cruel attraction
For his lack of ability to enact

So then she seeing the inevitable end
Unable her chastity anymore to defend
Gave up and gave in and gave him
All he desired by using her natural bent

Which as it came often it went
Away with a terrible smirk
Not having alas yet learnt
What it was to be the head of a Triumvirate.

IMPOSSIBLE

I dreamt that Octavio Paz was driving the car. We were talking casually about Victor Hugo and the drawings he would have done had he known the dramatic landscapes of Mexico... He is driving me towards a town — a village XOTL. A car follows us... It's the Bruho's cousin, he whispers, looking through the rear view mirror. Don't look now. When we arrive at XOTL the Bruho is a very aged and wrinkled André Breton. One hundred years old — says Octavio proudly. How did you get him here? I asked, amazed... Well, that's nothing, says Paz very modestly. We've done it for others. It's the least you can do for friends... Will you do that for me? I asked... Well, if you die before me. I'd commit suicide, if that's the case. Beware, says Octavio, it may not work. What works? I asked. Natural death — when the god takes you — not with your own hand. Meanwhile André Breton was fading... What's happening? I ask, alarmed. Nothing. He's just running out of energy... He'll be back tomorrow after five — and then you'll be able to question him on everything... Everything, I say — Yes, says Octavio confidently. He knows everything... The answer to all the riddles of the universe and existence. What fun, I say... The only thing is, will we be here tomorrow? You see tomorrow in this place is 100 years... ahead... I woke up feeling I knew... the truth: Octavio was in reality Carlos Casteñada and vice versa. Who had written whose books? — So what? said a voice. I recognized the voice of Victor Hugo... His hugeness was by my bedside bidding me farewell. He too, was now going to Mexico... for a vacation! Tired of Guernsey? I asked innocently. Oh, he said, I've forgotten the "Chants of Maldoror" and the author's letter. A certain Count de Lautreamont on a shelf in the kitchen. Surely that must be a pseudonym, I said, so it doesn't matter — one hundred years hence they will be found intact and the letter and the book will be read, your hugeness... But he was well on his way to Mexico, jump-roping over the enormous Atlantic waves.

THE MEN CAME

They did everything right
There was no error committed
The — well — the reason was that
All is well when we ask
When we answer all is tight —
Season it with something
Make it look nice
Don't ask anyone
Train your gun
To look inside
Spend less than you earn
Be stern.

Blood is among us
Don't let it leave now
Follow me and do as I do.

We arrived in clothing that morning

There were three of us. The men came in and
they did everything right. I was not requested
since their technical skill was well known.
The times were changing for the better. Yet
the worse was yet to come. The house repairs
went on as usual. They were pretty good at it.
I don't think there was anything seriously wrong.
However we went on as usual. Kept seeing
each other. The internals kept us
apart so that we would not be confused with
one another. There were some shops
for clothing — and women liked them for obvious
reasons. High tides, low spirits. Afternoons
the men left.
They did everything wrong
There was no reason to wait
Let's get out of here
Let them be sorry —

1986

GUN SMOKE

By sundown the slowdown begins
A thundering rain finds a roof
While the traveler starved for events
Meets the marriageable age in a root

However hold on to your credit
Which I trust you to be in good hands
And usually rally around
To reflect on what happened so fast

On the fringe of whatever may be
He stood up as early as dawn
And ruthless her gaze was upon him
But as yet no startling conclusion was drawn

Tonight let it be Lovenbrowning
Yet no conclusion was reached on whether
Something rusty had crawled out so early
As thinking in bed and breakfast for two

Who wants to be thought of as a fool.

FOR JORGE LUIS BORGES

Groussac grunting like a schoolboy appeared on scene. He sat down and eyed everybody as if they were mannequins. He looked angry, as only Groussac could ever be. She, on the other hand, never looked angry. She was always very pleasant. She looked as if she had just emerged from a novel by Groussac. Hm...

Groussac emerged from his Cadillac all clad in blue. He waved to his admirers and vanished inside the building. A classical elegance followed him around like a little dog. He appeared hurt, but not mortally: love was able to salvage him from the trash heap. This was no great feat, since he was already miles ahead of anybody else. Groussac didn't smell bad. He had around him the odor of time. No one knew why it smelt like lime.

Groussac could be one and many if he so wished. But his well-wishers wouldn't have any of it. For them Groussac was one, unalterable, unique, unrepeatable, single and singular. Yet Groussac knew that he was many, as many as they were who regarded him as one, in fact as one of them.

Groussac's skin, in spite of his 80 years, was as fresh as a daisy. How did he do it? When asked he enigmatically smiled back and cryptically added: "It's all thanks to Mr. Thomson." Everyone thought they knew who Mr. Thomson was — but alas the one he was referring to, was never mentioned.

Groussac in a way was horribly alive. Nobody seemed to mind. At his age this was considered scandalous. However, he could always pretend to be dead. Someone even signed his death certificate twice. But the judge didn't accept it. So Groussac went on being taxed for all kinds of ignominies — in spite of all his ingenuity in pretending — this, that or the other.

Why bother about Groussac? Who knows him today? Few people knew him better than Groussac himself. But he was forced to admit he knew very little — about himself and more on others. But since these others composed the very essence of Groussac, in a way he knew himself through them.

Being worried about Groussac was not easy. If encountered by accident or chance, although when Groussac was conceived there were no such things — he could be very grouchy. This grouchiness — was of the order of something like the 9th degree. Yet not to worry about it. He would change immediately if someone talked about Groussac.

This is the sea, said Groussac. And that was how nothing could ever become different. If the sea suddenly refused to be the sea — too bad for the sea. Groussac would insist and win through. The sea remained the sea in his eyes, and nothing else. Whoever dared contest such pronouncements was immediately declared a non-person. They ceased to exist in reality as conceived by Groussac.

1987

LONROT

The cry was heard every night
The hills shrunk, scared to death
The trees ran away, the roads twisted
Out of shape and out of sight
I'm dumfounded sitting before
A table with my head in my hands
Lonrot: the cry is repeated
And my hair drops off in anguish
I maintain a more or less straight
Line of thought although I swerve
In and out of Prussian Blue
And Bottle Green: notwithstanding
Pressure I press on: galloping hooves
Pound on the door: Angry fists, throw out
A handful of names: I call out Lonrot
I'm dredged to the last of our tomato juices
The house becomes suddenly dark
A storm is brewing — I know it, I feel it
And she is sitting in the armchair
Always with her dark glasses on
I feel it I know it: there's going to be
A terrible upheaval: Lonrot, Lonrot.

And this is not all. She lay on the bed.
She invited me to come in on top of her.
She felt my hair: she said dear boy —
You can let go now: Lonrot Lonrot
I feel that it's arriving
The pounding on the door
While we heave and moan
I mourn you every morning
I think it's all over now
She is feeling much better
How is she really: Lonrot?
Come what may
Stand up and fight.
Be yourself for once in our life: Lonrot.

And once more the world shrunk to zero size
Soon — if this were to go on — it would be
Just nothing to brag about — just an ordinary
Shriveling; it wouldn't take much
To accomplish: a small squeak — and pffft;
Lonrot — disappeared the name and the world
The name evoked: gone. And we who wrote this poem too.
Lonrot… Lonrot… Adieu…

3/14/87

LATE REMARKS

Romance roughs up at rush hour
Targets overcast primary concerns
Boredom makes death charge in disguise
Bespeckled prances home to admit
Marriage hastens flower by folly
Chastity enhances possibility
Being bothers bright-eyed brotherhood
Barnacles crowd out of town
Unvoiced muffler demonstrates conviction
Syndrome stiffens solitude
Sundown lifts up curtain and peeps
Play prolongs inmate dispositions
The voice gloves itself instantly
Shoemakers sprinkle Carthaginian on holidays
Ridiculous senses gravity below the belt
Repressed by Kodak replaced by comment
First breath drowns naked in bathtub
Matchmakers float on iridescent jokes
Fallacy has no dentist to fall Carthaginian on
Feet seldom betray the footsteps
Shoestrings hold on to lost man
Manifestly graced by all with nothing
Imports carefully to insist to meet
On impact they return the blow
Caution dances with dilemma's death
Mercury supports life out of order
Lightning bulbs eternity to pieces
Shreds assemble to assimilate late remarks
On arrival peaceful is predisposed
Validity tackles the sentence bravely
Parables make dullness vertebrate
Time barnacles before suicide.
Fearful fails to flower beforehand
Tables turned the fallen angel's disposition
The next page couldn't be delayed
This poem about to be written is somehow
Mysteriously connected to milk
This assumption will be somewhat difficult
To explore
Matrimony seems to be ennobled by adversity
Not in great quantities though

Repressed by Kodak

One's patch is often to pretend
The incorruptible
Who watches over all sentences
Has seen to it that they go on
Back to where they arrived
Without meaning to get them there.

The elbow will not jut out of anywhere.

A FLY BY NIGHT

Traveling on freeway 13 — I smelled a delicious Carthaginian and soon a beautiful enormous figure of a girl filled the horizon before me. She was coming closer and closer offering her lips until she passed through me or rather I passed through her. A little later another reclining figure sent out another perfume — she lifted her dress and showed her sex — I was driving right into it as she opened her legs. The sex came over me and vanished. Come with us and you will live forever — love is not dead — love never died. I began to wonder where these visions came from. They were enormous at a distance but when they came towards me they shrunk to normal size. A young man stood with his legs apart. I passed right under them. A girl did the same. There was a row of girls and males, teenagers in full bloom and beauty. Once again the phrases: "Come with us — we'll show you a good time. Don't forget to call 7777-111-112-2. We'll answer your calls personally." Love calls. Murmurs filled the air and a new perfume. Was I seeing things? A girl I had been together with saw visions. Perhaps I had been contaminated! What a predicament. Later clouds came and the figures became more sinister. There were people holding their eyes or their ears as if they heard terrible noises — or saw unbearable things. One man cut off his ear and ate it. Another bit his finger. Others opened their mouths as if in a silent cry. Some mingled, fought each other or made love. From afar they were enormous — when they came near, often inside the car they became tiny.

I was driving southwest to see some relatives in New Mexico — or Arizona. Night was falling and I was still in the desert among the mesas. No sign of any life or habitation — I still had 20 miles to go to the nearest town — called by the strange name of Dead Point. When I drove into Dead Point it lived up to its name. It was deserted. There was, however, a self-serve gasoline pump which took credit cards — I refilled. While I was refilling I felt a presence behind me. I turned. A colossal man was towering over me — a regular giant. His shoe was close to me. I leaned on it — it was solid. I looked up and it was the wall of a building with a giant poster. I had been leaning on a huge can — Now I was certain I was seeing things. Yet some doubt remained in my mind. I saw a light in a window above the gas pump. I called, "Anyone there?" No answer. I threw a pebble. Soon the window opened and an angry voice said, "Who is it?" The man leaning out of the window looked like a giant. "Where can I sleep?" I shouted. "There's a motel ten minutes away," was the answer, and the window closed with a bang that shook the whole building. Then the earth shook with a bang like a bomb exploding. I ran to the car and drove off in a relatively calm state of panic. The motel appeared in about 15 minutes in a cluster of trees. I parked and entered. The porter was half-asleep, but he woke up promptly when I appeared. "Room Sir?" "Yes." "Seven dollars plus service a night." I gave him the tip beforehand. He led me to the room. "This is our best," he said. It was spacious and the window had a view on the side of the road. "The *side* might come in the night," he said. "Don't take any notice, sir. They come and go. They are harmless." He separated the two syllables and made them sound like two words. Arm-less!

THE LAUGHTER OF THE GODS

Three Roman emperors approached me
We always think of the intruder
Even when we are not thinking
Of anything in particular —
My provisions on the table
Je les trouvé tres ennuyeux
Ils m'emmerdent a mourir
Ils sont même pas dangereux
I'm bored with their expressions
Of distaste and disapproval
They despise me — that I know
All three are peering down the well
In which I fuel at three o'clock
How they love to jeer and to make faces
But make haste my dear — don't linger
They may catch you unawares
And may rape you in the garden
By the path that leads to nowhere
In their arms you'll find the ecstasy
And the pain of early martyrs —
They will plunge their swords inside you
Intruders from another world —
Their desires are laws in action
They're cruel but also brave
Facing death at every moment
When their armies fall apart
Under the thrust of the barbarians
And of enormous elephants
Whether Greek or Carthaginian
They will fight until the last
Their soldiers will fall dead
They have nothing in their heads
Except battles and decrees
Some will wed their sisters
And sodomize their cousins
Some will kill their fathers
And will poison all their rivals
Often cuckolded by lusty wives
They'll behead them if they find them
In bed corpus delicto
Red handed with their lovers

No quarter then is ever given
Even if the gods do not agree
They'll be taken as they're given
As a whole — with a small part
In the nation's spoils departed
On their tombs will stand a phallus
Feathered like a pterodactyl
Well equipped to fly to heaven
To meet the gods at seven
O'clock in the afternoon
In an eternity of feasting
And of undying laughter

Yes they said — but do not be deceived
There is snow still on the mountain
And the rivers bear no flowers
On their watery backs —

Paris 6/23/88

Feathery Pterodactyl

MY BIRTHDAY POEM

The plain stretched out
The carriage ran its course
Dogs followed it and barked —
The chickens fled on both sides
Small settlements sailed by
Inside the round black carriage
Sat a round little man in black
The great dandylion
Journeying through thick and thin
To the ends of the earth
To where the end begins.
He bought and sold dead souls
He was a dead man's purchaser
He loved the condemned ones best
He bought them for nothing
He stepped barefooted in the snow
It was an exciting speech
And it made a strange noise
Finally it came to him
That he was entirely alone
And so were the two women:
And the dog also he left behind.
Nothing coming up
No love no help no money
No man helping anyone
They got cleaned out — their
Souls were cheap — strung up
In the market place
And they waited: the butterfly
Screamed the dogs moaned
The guardian of the peace barked.
They were all in the spirit world
For at least five minutes already.

California 5/7/89

66

LEFT BEHIND BY RECENT TASTE

Plagiarized by sound of fury
As Parisian as any café
Compromised by real words
Hollow sonnet poised to psych
Having eaten pink potato
Cooked with butter and mushroom sauce
Waters mouth above the palate
Tranquilized on food by taste
Laughed to halve the job in two
Cross the cris in jumps and starts
Mary Stuart makes a tart
Sometimes waiting mice
Hissing sounds of rising fame
In the valley traffic flows
Constant source of moneymaking
By the arm of justice naked
Sinclair could if Silicon prevailed
Upon following another's trade
Much is dust and must awake
A comic vein that laughs in vain
Foolish swamp of soapy cracks
Wordless romp destroys a fact
Windless, wordless, eyeless, timeless —
Forbidden to overstep their kindness
Funny foe of late lamented
Yet I'm always in the mood for (ants)
Sometimes caught without their pants
Panting seated rants to reach
Nothing naked loiters on the beach
Finger lately led to bring her
Must escape my old song

Instant help to hinder holder hence and hire
Doyens gather to divine the drunken view
Some have always something done to you
Others meant to fiction more than stretch the damaged pump
Reason randomly recalls what lover's levers spew —
Rancid with rural silence elbows graze below the belt
Grinding their way through iron shutters

GREAT EXPECTATIONS

I woke up this morning
It was raining it was cold
And I decided to stay home
And write this — Am I wrong?

∽

The least of my expectations
Is to live forever. Yet I feel
As if something inside me
Will survive me — and watch
And see what's going on after
I've left. It will be fascinating
To look at something
You're not supposed to see.

∽

Myself and others form
A consortium; our hands
Mingle we share our limbs
Our eyes see the same things
People walking in the street
Trains passing our ears listen
To sounds of traffic, rain, voices...
We conserve our impressions
On thin transparent threads...

It becomes us to be each other
And exchange selves when
Nobody is looking.

∽

I once asked you who you were
You answered: Nothing. I am nothing
Then when I insisted on learning
If you were from here or another place
You said: I'm here temporarily
Soon I will go to another country
Where? I asked, alarmed at the
Prospect of your departure. Nowhere
You answered: I'm going Nowhere
Where at last I will be somewhere.

∽

Your eyes belied your words:
You kept on saying you were sorry
But I saw clearly you were glad —
Very happy in fact to be or not to be
What you were. Your eyes were eloquent
Your mouth was very reticent indeed:
It never expressed anything: It just
Sat there and poured out leaves of grass
Which immediately grew tall on the floor
Hiding us from each other's view.

⤿

I said no — you said yes. Other people
Came between us. Some said no
Others said yes. These No's and Yeses
Stained the walls for those who
Would come later and stare and stare
Trying to guess to what to whom
Were addressed these "meaningless"
No's and yeses — so purely decorative
On the old walls of our dissentions.

⤿

Even if you didn't mean it the deed
Had been done; down there on the beach
Countless eyes had witnessed it: Indeed
What was it exactly you had done?
Which so changed your life and more?
I'm told many things — Yet it's hard for me to
Imagine the horrible scene
Let alone to connect it with what I know
About you and myself — as we emerge
From the sea only to sink back into
Each other's arms.

⤿

The army marched forward
No one looked back.
What was there to see?
The slate had been wiped clean.

Tabula Rasa. I was impressed
How could just a simple
Regiment marching in formation
Erase the landscape and all the people
The words you and I had said
Promises and vows and oaths sworn
We were supposed to keep forever?

∽

Anatomically your body
Is the same as mine: Some details
Are different. Yet these small changes
Became very perceptible at night
And now — we are centuries apart
For details have a way of growing
Taller and taller every day
Until their shadow falls
On everything we do on everything
We are — on everything we say.

∽

I'm not convinced that you are
Who you say you are. After all
We only met yesterday and
Already we are sharing secrets
Dogs, guns, wives, children, headaches
Crimes — beds, houses, ideas...
You sound so much like me

That I don't believe you exist —
Or better still — I have a hard time believing
I exist when you are around.
Yet we are both — branches of the same tree
Birds of a feather — flocking separately
Together.

1994

70

SULEIMAN THE MAGNIFICENT
A Peephole Into the Hot-to-a-man Hump-ire

Hurray for ODOAR NORSICUS — The sharpest blade in the Fermoth of Hysteria of the Best of the Est. In the beginnings there was a Firman — a Fir-man who descended from the high hills. I met Suleiman le Magnifique — walking down the avenue near the grocery shop. He bowed to me politely and ceremoniously — always wearing his splendid coat and superb turban — which was more like a wide border straw hat — than a tight fitting stretch of cloth. Suleiman the Magnificent was of course not anywhere near being an Ottoman. He was a Jewish kid — and his real name was Salomon, but he put on the art of a Turk — with panache and talent for impersonation. We soon became friends after a few encounters at the grocer's and he presented me to his sister Shula with whom he lived and who looked after him.

He had a weasel face and closely slit eyes. He was no oriental. Perhaps Indian or Mexican. I asked him, breaking the rules. Indonesian, he answered. I had been wrong. He was from the orient — a kind of orient. I sat on the bed and pondered for a while. Then I lay down, turned off the light. As I was sinking, I heard voices, and then a louder shouting — a door banged — someone was knocking on mine. I hesitated, half asleep. "Who is it?" I said. "Open up," said a desperate voice, "or he'll get me." "Who will get you?" "The man in…" she mumbled something. "What man?" "The man in blue," she blurted out. "Quick, please, open." Reluctantly I went to the door and opened it with the chain still on — just to make sure it wasn't some kind of trick. I saw her. It was the girl of the sky earlier. "You," I said. "How did you come to be…" "Quick," she said, "before he catches up." I opened the door and as let her in I saw his shadow — hastily I locked it. There was a laugh. "You believe I can't come in," said the voice in a whisper. "Well you'll see… I go through doors, walls, windows, roofs, floors — Never mind — now — later — you'll see." She stood there trembling looking crazed. "Who are you?" I said. "I don't know," she said, "who are you?" "You must be joking," I said. "No," she said, "I'm not joking. I've forgotten who I am, was…" It was Shula. But it wasn't her. And she wasn't thinking of seducing me to bed. She was beside herself with fear and desire. She was dead. She loved to be dead. And with her the HOT-O-MAN UMPIRE collapsed. She lifted her skirt and showed me her sex. And we had sex both alive and dead. Suleiman the Magnificent took off his turban and looked on appreciatingly. The marriage was magnificent. And we lived happily ever after. Our grandchildren were half Greek and half Turkish. We so love our enemy.

CONVERSATION WITH ECKERMAN I

That morning he couldn't come.
Herr Doctor Freud had foreseen it all.
I waited in vain. I heard someone
Climbing the stairs. They knocked
At another door. I'm disappointed
I had so much to tell him.
But it is well known that at some
Point counter transference — occurs: And
The relation of patient to therapist
Acquires a negative turn. Maybe
That's what happened — How could
He have guessed so much in retro-
spect! He was an honorable man
And honorable men are rare.
I must cherish him in spite of
Anything that might happen —
What if he throws a chair at me
Or a cup? What if he throws an apple!
That would be the end. Chairs, cups,
I don't mind — but an apple is a mortal
Insult — I would never forgive him that.
If that happened I would dunk him
With hot tea — even if it burns him
Let him have a foretaste of hell
Who cares. Am I behaving badly
I hadn't realized how desperate
I was for conversation. And not
With anybody. I'm very choosy
You know. I don't accept substitutes.
If you think I'm an old bore — you may
Be right — but I too have my rights
And my wrongs — I'd disavow
God himself if he came down
To wash my hair with his feet.

1994

72

CONVERSATION WITH ECKERMAN II

For God anything is possible
We humans are so limited by
Nothing — Sorry I meant to say
Nothingness — slip of the tongue
I know what you are thinking
That I'm a megalo — That I must
Believe I'm God — Oh where is
This man? He could tell me
So many great things about
My state of mind without ever
Making me angry — How I long for him —
What's that? I thought I heard footsteps
A knock at the door — it's not possible
My dear friend you're here after all
You've come in spite of hail or sunshine
What joy. Sit down. We'll have some tea
Or coffee... No, no, it's no bother —
I'm so delighted to see you — you know
Madonna said something yesterday
On TV about how she knew a song
Had ended! She felt a tingling in
Her toes — Yes, I'm tingling — isn't that
"A gas?" I'm feeling that right now —
So I must end this poem — alas —
Abruptly — I don't know whether
I'll see her again on the moon or on TV
But what does it matter, I've taped her —
So whenever I feel the urge — I'll press
A button — and then press on for an advantage
In spite of my age: My dear Faust.

1995

SITTING, READING

She was sitting reading a book in the library.
She was reading a book. It was her I was sure it
was her. She was reading a book. Yes she was reading.
It was her. It was almost certain that it was her. In
those days I had lost a woman for whom I cared a lot.
I had seen her among other women, in a group
of women. She stood out like a dark star from all
the rest. It was her. I'm sure it was her. She fit the
description. What description? Had I been given a
description? There was no description available.
How come I knew it was her? I had no clue. No
Certainty. What could I do? I couldn't go up to
her and say. Is it you? Are you her? She would answer
Who are you? And then maybe she would add, who
are you looking for? Maliciously, intentionally
Like a dark star she stood out among the other
readers in the library. She was so remarkable. In
those days I had lost a woman I cared for more
than my own life. She was sitting reading a book in
the library. In the huge library she was sitting reading
a book. An open book on the table in front of her. She
was not reading the book. She was dreaming. She was staring
at me from over the book in a furtive manner. I knew
it was her. She knew I was he. We knew we were
we. We both knew. But did I know I was me? Did
she know I was me... Who did she think she was? Who
did we think we were? Were we the ones who were
meant to be we? To be me? To be her? To be... us?

They Too Were Reading

RHETORICAL FIGURES

I have two of these books
Which of the two belongs to me?
To whom do I belong?
To you of course how could
It be otherwise
Imagine how tired I can be
By opposing arguments
I like refining my point of view
Until it is elongated so sharply
That it becomes
A kind of nec plus ultra
Accompanied by a factotum
I believe most people
In their peculiar energies are versions
Of each other — and/or
Remain faithful to each other
By being what they are:
Not just by themselves
But all together huddled in one corner —
Made to think what they are and what
They are not what they really want to be
But only pretentious pretexts
And high gloating farcical poseurs
Reflecting others in their eagerness
To be themselves — solid enough
So that they can hang on indefinitely
But this alas is not the only thing
Possible to them — they can also
Be nothing else but — We have
To give a few more examples
To fill in the appropriate
Slots — for no slobberer was he who…

THE PIANIST AND THE OTHER MAN

Many years ago I composed a poem
Which I lost — It was called
The pianist and the other man
It spoke of a curious contest
Between him who turns the pages
Of a musical score
For him who plays the instrument
And slowly the meaning
Of the ordinary scene
Becomes ominous — They
Were not collaborating, but
Competing who would
Get there first — the finishing line
Where the musical sound
And the notation end
The one who turned the pages
Faster and faster was becoming
Pale with frenzy — while the
Pianist — well he banged away
With trills and accords and nimble
Melodies — as quickly as his fingers
Would allow him — In the end
Because there was an end
To this endless competition
Both of them collapsed —
The pianist with his head
On the keyboard — and
He who turned the pages
Slumped over the grand piano
The instrument of their
Desperate bid to get there first.

1971-1996

TORQUE

More news from elsewhere from nowhere, from
I wish I had a book of quotations handy
to jot down once again all this nonsense
this gibberish — this sexless
rubbish which arrives from
the Other World — The one
our ancestors named Shady
Hades — our enemies who
killed and massacred
us as we ventured
out of doors into
the fields which
once were ours
but now bewa-
re of these
bastards
who make us
slave, day
and night
for them
to drink
and eat
your flesh
and blood
usurpers
of the mansion
of the Mas-
Ter.
Ah!
Men-
In Aida.

AS I SAT WRITING

I wrote all day all over the early morning
I wrote the night all over the table
I wrote the crickets into the night
I wrote the kitchen into the house

I wrote the house into the vast plantation
On whose grounds three roads are coming and going
I wrote a town at the end of one of the roads
I wrote in a girl waiting at a corner café

Writing me a letter which I will receive
If I ever manage to write in the post-office box
In my unfinished town — I now write
Under a lamp in a hurry because I have written the sun down

Below the western horizon of trees — on which I have written
The parakeet's screeching and a barking of dogs
And I also wrote the songs the natives were singing
Into your ears as they come out of their mouth

And I wrote of the world as impossible
To live in — I write myself out of it slowly
Carefully, in calligraphic handwriting and I send it to God
Whom I've just written out of ink so that he can't

Answer me if yes or no the world
Has been written on a permanent basis
On the endless scroll of creation
Exhibited in the garden of the old mosque

By a dealer to a visitor from another country
Who is no other but me and who threatens to buy up everything
And hang it on the wall of the verandah of the house
In which just now I was sitting and writing all this
off the top of my head.

THE ULTIMATE EMPEROR

Empty my soul
Empty my head
Emptying every living stone
Emptiness surrounds me
I feel comfortable in it
Human presence would
Be embarrassing: Let's forget
About humans — Titus Livius
And live in the aloneness
Of empty rooms, mansions
And other kinds of
Solitude — You and I alone
On a bench in Tuscany
And I will forsake Rome
And also the Empire
I will erase them all from
My slate — I've already
Signed an edict authorizing
A total massacre of the
Inhabitants of the known
World — Then you and I
Titus Livius will be really
Alone — For our Legions
I will arrange another
Kind of death by mutual
Suicide. They'll have orders
To die either by the famous
Plant that killed Socrates
That demonic man or else
By the sword — Then Titus Livius
You and I will be the absolute
Rulers of the world — but
Eventually you too will
Have to die — before me —
So that in my last
Days of triumph
I will taste the world
Utterly alone — before
I join you in the Halls
Of Hades where all the
Shadows of the living go.

1996

80

A Shadow of the Living

EXPERIMENT

Searching for my own books in the future...
In the unsmiling corridor of the huge library
The endless rows of small books stored
Stacked to the ceiling all
In alphabetical order. In these
I am searching for myself in vain.
Nowhere to be found my works in writing;
Now even in the heads of those who read
All night with shaded lamps shivering in over-coats
I suffer from the chill of not being anywhere near
Where they who matter to me are...
Through endless libraries I wander seeking
Searching, following the trail of letters, of tears
In the fabric of appearances
Subjects, format, dates; no living
Creature inhabits those dismal vistas
Stretching towards nowhere known
No form agreeable to the eye appears
Behind walls and walls of books
One day they will be set on fire. It happened before.
Only a few sentences will remain on living lips
Maybe a word or two of what was written
With fear and trembling with hopes and expectation
That in the future they'll inhabit
The eyes the breasts the mind the bodies
Of innumerable future explanations
Who will dream of me and wish I were there
To answer live questions about protocol I wish I were
Among them aware of what for them I suffered
How I wrote about this great commotion, this
Sound of nothing tearing the skin off
The face of things.

FOR MOE MOSKOWITZ AN EXEMPLARY
BOOKSELLER.

In my Century
Astronomy was still
In its infancy
And so was space travel
My contemporaries
Still pondered in vain
On the mystery of how
The Universe began
And how it will end
And there were no big news
On cancer, AIDS, heart
Disease and old age...
All these still plagued
Humanity since Adam and Eve
Since Noah's Ark
And Pandora's box
In this my century
In which I was born
A gentle heart
A bookseller died
Who was indefatigable
Selling buying and trading
Books and jokes
(Always in good humour)
With customers, old and young,
Seldom losing his cool
Loved by all — I asked him once

How he was — and he answered
Apart from some major problems
I'm fine — he was kind
And compassionate
To those whom needed to go
To the bathroom — a rarity
In Berkeley — loved by all
Except perhaps by some book-traders
Under his busy and gruff manner
Expediting business
Ringing up sales
Neutralizing magnetic charges
Next, next... Whose next?

And the flow of books
Ran through his hands
And those of his assistants
Smoothly a mighty river
On some days, a trickle
At other times
In this 4 story bookstore
On Telegraph Avenue
All through the Middle
And the end of my Century
And I too sometimes
In my book or human form
Went in and out of the store
Within easy reach
In and out of print
In my own personal Century
Still so ignorant about

The beginning or the end
Of the Universe —
A gentle and kind bookseller
Moe Moskowitz — he will be truly
Missed and dearly remembered.

Berkeley, the Mediterranean Café, April 10th, 1997.

EVERY NIGHT I DREAM

Every night I dream of great poetry
Quite different from mine
Or what I will ever write
And yet — every night I dream
Of this very different poetry
Composed of lines so solid
So dense and grainy
They could have been made of granite
I ask myself — what is their subject
What do they say these marvelous lines
Which to behold — will leave you aghast
They'll take your breath away
But — however — in any case — I'm sorry to say
Impossible to guess what it's all about
And I have tried and tried, believe me,
And puzzled over these lines
Day after day — and in the night
They keep on coming back
With new earthshaking and tremendous
Messages — of great import
That everyone should hear
But not a single word remains
When I open my eyes — they're gone
They vanish in pure daylight
These huge edifices — those titanic
Workings of each night.

9/17/96

OTHER BOOKS BY NANOS VALAORITIS

Poetry in Greek:
Verse: The Punishment of the Magi, 1947
Central Arcade, 1958
Anonymous Poem, 1974, 1978
Nests of Microbes, 1977
Hero of the Accidental, 1979
Featherly Confession, 1982
Poems I & II (collected), 1983, 1987
The Bottom Line, 1984
The Coloured Stylograph, 1986
Anideograms, 1996
Sun Executioner of a Green Thought, 1996
Allegorical Kassandra, 1998
Descent of the M, 2002
Alphabet of the deaf mute, 2003

Prose in Greek:
Traitor of the Written Word, Ikaros, prose 1980
Diamond Tranquilizer, Tram, 1981
Some Women, Themelio, 1982 (won State Poetry Prize)
Bones of the Greeks, a novel, Themelio, 1982
The Assassination, a novella, Themelio, 1984
The Treasure of Xerxes, a novel, Hestia, 1984
The Talking Monkey, Aigokairos, 1986
Paramythology (three collected prose texts), Nefeli, 1996
God's Dog, narratives, Kastaniotis, 1998
The Broken Arms of the Venus de Milo, a novel, Agra, 2002

Essays in Greek:
Andreas Embirikos, 1988
Ypsilon, For a Theory of Writing, Exantas, 1990.
Modernism, the Avantgarde and Pali, Kastaniotis, 1997 (won State
Prize for Testimonies)

Poetry in English:
Hired Hieroglyphs, Kayak, 1970
Diplomatic Relations, Panjandrum, 1971
Flash Bloom, Wire Press, 1980
My Afterlife Guaranteed, City Lights, 1990
Anthology of Greek Poetry, translated and edited with Thanasis
Maskaleris, Allegro Shwartz, *et al,* Talisman House Publishers, 2003

Poetry in French:
Mon Certificat d'Eternité, Digraphe, 1996
Executeur d'une Pensée Verte, L'Harmattan, 1998

Forthcoming:
Tropology of the Concrete, Pandora's Box, I & II
Homer and the Alphabet, For a Theory of Writing II.

ABOUT THE AUTHOR

Nanos Valaoritis was born of Greek parents in Lausanne, Switzerland in 1921 but grew up in Greece. He studied Classics and Law at the University of Athens, English Literature at London University, followed by courses in Mycenian Grammar with Michel Lejeune at the Écoles des Hautes Études of the Sorbonne. He moved to London in 1944, where he translated Modernist Greek poets of the 1930's, while contributing articles in Cyril Connolly's *Horizon* (1946) and translations for John Lehman's *New Writing* (1944-1948). He also edited and translated *The King of Asine* (1948), a selection of poems by George Seferis with Bernard Spencer and Lawrence Durrell. He was to meet many poets in London's literary community, such as T.S. Eliot, Stephen Spender, W.H. Auden, and Dylan Thomas, and worked for Louis MacNeice at the BBC. In 1954 when he moved to Paris, he met Andre Breton and participated in the activities and meetings of his Surrealist group until 1960, when he returned to Greece, where he edited the avant-garde review *Pali* (1963-1967). He was to leave Greece a year after the Junta came to power in 1967.

In voluntary exile from the repressive junta, Nanos began his American life teaching at San Francisco State University in both the Creative Writing and Comparative Literature Departments. Since his retirement in 1993, he has published a remarkable body of work, including books of poetry, poetic texts, short stories, novels and novellas, essays, translations and anthologies co-edited, spending part of each year in California and the rest in France and Greece. In 2004 he was awarded the prestigious prize for poetry from the Athens Academy of Letters and Science in recognition of his life's work. He was also awarded a gold medal of honor by the President of Greece. Nanos is married to the American Surrealist painter Marie Wilson.